THE BLACK CONDITION
FT. NARCISSUS

THE BLACK CONDITION FT. NARCISSUS

jayy dodd

Live! From Wilderness Records

(Some Place Not Here, USA, 2Oi7)

Nightboat Books
New York

Copyright © 2019 jayy dodd

All rights reserved

Printed in the United States

ISBN: 978-1-937658-97-7

Design and typesetting by HR Hegnauer

Text set in Perpetua and Helvetica

Cataloging-in-publication data is available from the Library of Congress

Nightboat Books

New York

www.nightboat.org

SIDE A

SIDE B

BONUS TRACK

Being consulted as to whether the child would live a long life,
to a ripe old age, the seer with prophetic vision replied
"If he does not discover himself."

Metamorphoses Book III
(A. S. Kline's Version) 339-358
"Echo sees Narcissus"

What's the nastiest shade you've ever thrown?
Existing in the world.

Juliana Huxtable

SIDE A

narcissus

(demo)

if even in the mired river / you can be enamored / by your own
reflection / it is because you are still a partial-god — how else to
make sense / of divining affected desire / for a sight less temporal
than a ghost — seeing oneself / can be a dream realized — though
i have always had more faith / in fantastic things unseen.

I Know I Been Changed

After Lashun Pace (Rhodes)

no longer can you call me a beast of this earth
this tender flesh is not satisfied by the harvest
in my mouth — now abundant — milk & honey
i've crossed barren waste for holier land
because i am an angel now
the blood of my body made snow-white robe,
all-gilded miracle, my new language is flight
at my shoulder blades, an expanding
without ache — wide as freedom
this body prophesied transfiguration
called itself: divine, called the streets: alabaster
called baptism: the afternoon

i ain't what it used to be, made new
made sacrament & fear
no longer confined to sensations or consequence
no longer concerned about the failings of mortality
     i know i been changed & you can't tell me no better
you will call me out my-self, blasphemous
but i have heard on high my body is harmonic gospel
it was written in sacred memory before coming into being
now, i am here ready for rapture, cause
     the angels in Heaven done signed my name
     i said, the angels in Heaven done signed my name

narcissus, away from the river

all the girls at the party
look better than me

& i'm proud. (i'm embarrassed)
sometimes i believe they are too,

embarrassed i mean,
for me. or

i'm invisible.

> *does this dress*
> *make me look*
> *real?*

there are all of the girls

[thick-slim-slimthick-thickthick,
ebony-tan-sand-mahogany-chestnut,
highfemme-lowbutch-heels-kicks,
afros-yaki-lacefront-contour-vaseline]

of all the girls on the dancefloor,

my skirt is hiked up the highest,
i'm the sweatiest. watch out for my hands.

i am the most beautiful broken clock tower,

catch me real right every so often.
otherwise,

see me a baffling machination.

shade is a time of day
& fierce

animals can often see in the dark.

all the girls at the party know this look

is called   *trying my best.*

the boys
see through me —

i'm invisible.

though one stopped
after looking all night

& said how beautiful my skin was. so that was nice.

this other passed me a blunt
& asked me about my junk.

is it conceited to believe
when dudes interrogate
my skirt

they   *trying to fuck?*

or maybe i want to imagine myself
that kind of attractive.

Put Your Hands Your Where My Eyes Can See

after Busta Rhymes

Bitch

nigga —

as in, real clockable
       from across the room
a question mark   what part
of me punctuates best?

is you feeling
       how i'm feeling
            really, truly though?

if you question   my inspection
tell it to me slow.

i know your kind
is incline
to tell it to my
throat.

but you seen   that I'm mean
don't wanna be exposed.

scared

to

death —

i'm scared of this kind of command.
telling you to expose yourself

when you have already seen me   bare.
i only un-know what happens between your eyes &

my own conceits.   i'm as scared
of being ignored as i am of being seen.

please put your hands where my needs can see them
open palm, fit me, my waist,

if you really   wanna party   with me

i'll be in the corner trying to catch
the/ here or there /light reflecting from my phone.

i have been called elusive.
admitting its purpose feels like revealing

how an illusion works.
as if there is magic in fear, or

being consumed by fluorescent dread,
as everyone around you lifts their hands to the sky.

act
fruity
yo —

but if i caught ya here

must have
seen me
looking
real right.

in the
back of
your mind,
got ya
pants tight.

if you ask
i'll make you
& your friends' night.

     this is my fantasy though,
     all my barking, is rooted
     in fear of you realizing
     i wanted this before
     even entering the room.
     i wanted you,
     before you,
     to spot me a blooming
     succulent. call this look
     a ripening.   pick me,
     dripping in my dew.
     slopping up the cool of the night.
     trust i will flower in your hand.

narcissus #17

the wild pack of dogs are speaking to each other / tonight / my room echoes / brown 40-ounce bottles / told someone the night-time here sounded like Texas / i thought cicada was a type of tree / the buzzing still comes from the land / a humid hanging / what is the weather suppose-t'be like? / my bones cry weary demanding the sun & i disavow their ache as penance / my own worst case scenario / shuddering from high ground about the danger of floods / every water i've known has been ocean / met a lake & opened my eyes underneath / i would be lying if i said i knew this land / when everything here is present / i just imagined myself in agreement / now in the mirror, whispering: *you're alive* / speaking to my reflection as if it would know better than i about the unreal / *you think i don't see you* / nothing about this is supposed to make sense / this is all barking to the moon / the only face i can speak to honestly / even my reflection knows this mouth is a false prophet / disillusioned to believe my lips holy / what humor / what arrogance / i keep the water beside me to see myself in it / all this, a drowning / disoriented & swallowing constantly / i feel as i am caught maw agape / reeking of all i have potential for / nothing is going to sound its best here / this is an itching of a feral evening's stupor / the night keeps its frequency on right now / every so often / taking a break / to remind me / it knows i listen.

narcissus in spring time

I fiend so, for touch
when my fingertips,
grace the cashier,
from behind
the bullet-proof glass,
at the liquor store;
I quiver & contort
all the way home.

This is the first
vernal equinox
I have not actively
wanted to die.

     Inactively,
my dying
feels like a constant.

What percent
of my fresh air
is tar & nicotine?

The metaphor
between seasons
& death
is more dead
than my desire
to be such.

The sky is so wide now,
it keeps every-one
in its expanse.

This, the first inauguration
of spring
I have not
wanted to wilt.

The first harvest
the budding daffodils
did not elicit
a madness.

The unfurling
gasps of my lungs
more consistent
than the breeze.
Not every climate
calls for ritual.

Yet, every hand
laid upon me
feels better
than my own.

Manual

(Manualis)

Hand-Me

Hand-This

Hand-That

Hand-Here

Hand-Up

Hand-Down

Hand-High

Hand-Low

Hand-Off

Hand-To

Hand-Back

Hand-Held

Hand-Gun

Hand-Cuff

Hand-Blade

Hand-Of-God

Hand-To-God

Hand-That-Feeds

Hand-To-Hand

Hand-To-Mouth

Hand-Choke

Hand-Grab

Hand-Over-Heart

Hand-Over-Fist

Hand-Hip

Hand-Thigh
Hand-Under-The-Table
Hand-Warm
Hand-Cold
Hand-Ache
Hand-Love

    Hand, Red
    Hand, My
    Hand, Black

(Labor)

My momma ain't never been above hard work. She come from
    sharecroppers.
Enslaved niggas. A lineage of labor. Took eighteen hours for me.
    She say she so proud
cause she ain't never seen her boy without a job.

But she ain't never seen my hands calloused, either. I know so
    little of hard labor,
I have found offices & noose-tie casual wear as comfort —
been an experienced-nigga, having long understood economy.

Niggas always marvel at my hands. Like how they so soft.
The hardest thing I did as a child was dance. These hands have
    always been
soft things. The signal to the otherwise unaware, how my work is
    required to hold me.

(Litany)

What if God was something
that could be held in the hand.
With us here. A present thing.
Birth now a heavenly place.

Here, hold close the divine.
We, a people to be held.
Hands to God, we entangle
ourselves together.

Our instructions simple:
hold one another close.
This is neighbor & lover & kin.
We hold each other, as possible.
Too soon — a trespassing.

Un-burden our hearts.
All this a manicured chorus,
high above. Pour out, feed us.
We grow new & whole again.

First, wear a white linen suit. Black linen Shirt. Black loafers.
Five-dollar sunglasses from the Garment District.
Hold court. This is a commencement.
Or, a blue suit. Ill fitting, but filled. Final interview.

> The shot will come from no-where. Your hands a-flailing.
> Miracle wound & you, the assassinated, *right?*.

Or, lay still in your bed. Naked. They will find you,
beautiful. You, a rest. Your skin soft as ever, just now
cold. Hear them tell it. Speak of you as you are.
Isn't that your favorite lament?

(Manicure)

acrylics from down the street — *black matte*, this time.
my thumbs are blistering. before they a calloused,
swollen thing stained in turmeric & my mother asks about
my smoking. I tell her it's not what she thinks, but I guess it is from
the lighters. stubborn, now split & peeling. my hands

are soft pretty gifts from my mother. the blistering,
my own stubbornness. but I keep them delicate & soft
other-wise. girls always tell me how my nail-beds are beautiful.
how pretty my fingers look.   my mother is
often taken with how pretty how my hands look
when I hold things.

(Play)

Hand me a man in my hands
    & I will hold that man.
He will be man-handled.
For I know how to handle a man.
My hands have handled men.
Men know my hands.
Men have caught my hands.
Men have held my hands.
I have held men in my hands.
Men mind being held
    & I hand-hold them.
Hands-held together.
Holding back.
Men holding men back with hands held up by other hands.
Hand me a man's hand
    & I will hold him, like healing is possible in the palm of a hand.
Hold me, please, your hands —
    a haven, a holding pattern hovering over my mine.
Hold my hand, hold me, in your hand I am a small
    & playful thing.
Hand me myself, hold me to man.

(Manually)

I've imagined these hands a liberation,

dreaming of a swallowing universe.

Holding here & now,

I remember how the body cannot choke itself.

Still, there are other ways of betrayal.

Out-side of the body. A power in the hands:

before these muthafuxkers take you out

Taking. A life. Taken. The body preys itself — handled.

Held. These hands caught up. Catch freedom.

narcissus in dystopia

after MAA

the bees within us could die at any moment

                                  something more empty than holding

everything is becoming background noise

                                  barren streams with ashes of blossoms

i hope the drones would find me sleeping

                                  there is no palace in sterile fantasy

with my computer open i believe in radiation

                                  to bear myself a queen requires more

waves contract & exhale my reflection

                                  while there are never crowns in dystopia

                                  there are only lakes or oceans or rain

maybe one of these frequencies will work

                                  unrecognizable in toxic disfiguration

against the drift i consume this static rippling

                                  what still buzzes in the sky

all possible torrents can still be corrupted

                                  beyond this hive of half lives:

the day is ambient — the night is garbled

                                  messages from the matter we-are-made-of

pops & hisses travel light-years

                                  a future darker than here

just to speak of the void

———————

                 the last place my archaic transmission stares back

daybeat (interlude)

can't tell me nothing bout myself
cause there are too few words
for the this-here anyway.

despite all cosmetic possibilities
place-held-hollow in the fantastic.

today's beat is gilded
in lilac-nipplebrown-nude.

the lips pout their intimacy
secret & slick.

having never felt the cloak of night
as more than still reveling
my own transparence —

                there is no time of day
                this body cannot fail.

how differently do we dress ourselves
in loss.

i attempt to beat a kind-beauty
into my forever or

                what if this look is my last?

Lyrebird

i wish my mouth
told you less about chainsaws
my song   a buzzing now —
this the only squawk i know.
after my sprawling: a groove.   i wait
for a mate to meet me until then   my lament:
a camera shutter.   my screech only knows what it hears
i can gab to all the other birds in native hoots make my own kind
unsure of my gawking plumage. yet   this is the only caw to keep me going
stand in the clearing, a bushel & leaf stage   hear my range   warbles & trills.
this beak a barreling of bulldozers   of a throat   built for spectacle.
a call   from habitat unnatural.   mechanics whiz
an unmistakable static   beneath my breast-bone.   almost
a mocking.   beneath my feathers are klaxons.
oh, to be a siren?   wouldn't that be beautiful:
to reply back to the sky
a more appealing
coo.

in(t)elegance: a conspiracy theory

you can make almost a million dollars by killing one angel outside
his house / the deep state is located in a police locker-room / they
plan war games over dinner / this is not a lie.

this could be a lie, but our destruction is definitely an inside job /
or at least CIA-funded.

they build super-predator soldiers out of crack & dollar bills / hang
them out to dry in the street   for (4) hours.

a Black man can be assassinated sleeping in his bedroom, shot next
to his wife & unborn / a Black girl can be taken, sleeping on her
Grandmothers' couch / these aren't lies / these aren't accidents /
those aren't images or illustrations between the lines / living Black
is a federal offense.

some free handouts   from my government name:
the prison industrial complex can melt steel beams
the alt-right killed JFK.

every sleeper cell in Amerikkka is a group of white boys watching /
The Daily Show, trying not to masturbate to each others' inadequacies.

the conspiracy is calling it art instead of news / declaring life is an
act / of terrorism.

your house is not your home unless it is secure / this is a lie.
your house is not your home unless it is on fire / this is lie.
your house is never your home, all you have is the fire.

they don't teach us the real reason we never sing the last verse
of the national anthem / slavery wasn't so bad if you profited
from it / Black people are always late because we are stuck
in the middle of the ocean, indefinitely.

the world is scheduled to end yesterday / the doomsday clock
doesn't consider colored people time / we've already lived through
an apocalypse.

but this is all a simulation / run by a select group of endangered
lizards who control the stock / exchange / this could be a lie.

facts are meant to be broken, rules are meant to be disproved truth
can be tailored with the right measurements / tongues can be cut
with the right language / lives can be stolen with the right history.

language is the last organic thing to grow on the planet / all things
/ can still name themselves Arbitrary / this is not a lie / which
common sense do you use here? / does this not resemble what you
call nonsense? / all to disguise such treacherous imagery.

assume every camera has already taken your face / plastered it on
the wall, writes your name in its journal, doodles hearts around
your visage / this is a lie / but every camera does identify you by
your bad side / on a tiny screen in an undisclosed location / the
panopticon is being updated.

it's a madness constantly looking over your shoulder only to find /
a void / they listen to how you speak to yourself & make sure / all
messages are transmitted.

it is in the water / it is in the wires / it is in the air
filter the rain / everything is contaminated.

our immune systems are failing / the land can't call in sick

there has to be something hurdling toward us that we don't now
know about / dear sky of midnight mass, we ask your devastation
strike us down.

the moon landing wasn't staged, but NASA has been colonizing
since the 60's / all the Martians are on reservations & Venusians are
being brought over by the spaceship-load.

we missed the first contact by looking at the wrong abyss THEY
were already here / THEY already left / THEY didn't like what
they saw / THEY found all the undetonated bombs WE left
scattered / around the house & realized WE are the savagest in the
galaxy.

the Earth is not flat / though I couldn't tell you differently this a lie /
satellites are real. they hover, ghosts / above a hostile atmosphere.

say three Hail Mary's & cover your heart in aluminum foil.
the communion wine is locally grown from gentrified soil. but,
Bread Inc. has subsidized the body of Jesus.

too much of the food we eat is plastic / this is not a lie.
there are wood-chips in your parmesan cheese
gum chewers are 14 times as likely to have a mound of play-doh /
the size of a tennis ball in their stomachs / this is a lie.

the water is safe to drink / not sure how the truth works here
the water was safe to drink today, but last week it was not. this
is not a lie.

the water needs to be tested / not sure how pipes work here / the
water needs to be tested again, but it has returned / to previous
levels / of acceptable contamination. this is not a lie.

they have poisoned whole cities / this is not a lie.
they don't want liberty or justice for y'all / this is a lie
they sell liberty & justice, but it's a ponzi scheme
of identity politics & the "real" working class.

there is no civility in democracy / they want you to believe your
votes count / they want you to not be able to vote.
they are trying every way to count you out

a watchlist grows of those who won't survive in Amerikkka.

narcissus (dream 002)

when i can't sleep through the night, i make fists of my sheets.
　　like grabbing all the money i'm owed.
it's hard to be worth the world's weight in cool.
why do i feel guilty believing i deserve to eat good?
i just wanna feed all the lovers i reject & still have time to be alone.
i sleep better with someone else but the conceit of my condition
　　is to placate restlessness.
i don't deserve the gold, or pearls, or rose quartz.
i am worth my weight in water, in ire, in numb limbs.
i wanna be (rich or) in love.
i wanna die either comfortable or happy.
i wanna sleep through the night without having to feel myself
beneath the bedcovers —
　　sopping wet with the only excess i know.

The Subject Was ~~Faggots~~

After Gil Scott-Heron

& the quote was:

down there them

~~niggas~~ be ~~faggots~~

~~niggas~~ be ~~faggots~~

~~niggas~~ be ~~faggots~~ be ~~niggas~~ be ~~faggots~~

who living

puff, pass, sip, pass, puff,

smoke-evenings in darkroom

with just enough light for eye-contact

at Milwaukee & Woodward

grinding & drinking & laughing.

trying their best to see

the shade, the seething, the sickening looks

of desirable longing who were in the club.

checking for something better.

something better than being ~~niggas~~.

something better than being ~~faggot~~.

~~faggot-niggas~~ check for something better.

check for you, check that lip.

these are the corner-you-in-the-bathroom ~~niggas~~,

the size-queen-you-up ~~faggots~~,

& i mean i just had to take it

to dig it.

my crowning attraction is my height

& the myth of long, long limousine between

my long, long evening scowl. yet, i again wilt,
crush swan feathers of manhood in my thighs.
but hiding in the corner behind the excuse
of a stall, i feared for my dick & his,
uh, her, or *its* safety.
had there been no sign saying men's room, i might
not have felt the need to expose myself. i might
not have become this unsatisfactory subject
& WHO KNOWS what could have gone down.

faggot rap

ghazal remix

(verse one)
when the children's eyes wonder on this here faggot
prepare their lips / remind them to not fear faggots

some histories never allow our true flames to burn
yet / present futures show they'll still sear faggots

the agenda left us behind / though it was never clear
since them homophiles never went near faggots

left us to blood-sick boil in our own skin
too austere to adhere to mere faggots

all this / some dream of every up & coming legend
slay the day / for the down by the pier faggots

if my taking in the air / we share / leaves you breathless
i am unflinching as i am unamused / a real severe faggot

audacity is in / no time to blend / the only passing is time
now appear / giving a cheer / for the cavalier faggots

all around / we abound / there will always be faggots
we hope to provoke / being wild / free faggots

subject your gaze / fashion likable suspect
become too clockable cause y'all oversee faggots

under watch we form ourselves a mystery,
that's the key to ID as authentically faggot

the question of choice is will of ignorance,
who would masquerade as a wannabe faggot?

we all agree / this being is about seeming unseen
yet this world is ending / ask the absentee faggot

(refrain)

so / faggot-faggot / what's the faggot-faggot tea?
how should a faggot-faggot / faggot-faggot be?

see / faggot-faggot / see / faggot-faggot / see
be faggot-faggot / be faggot-faggot / be

live / faggot-faggot / live faggot-faggot free
go / faggot-faggot / go / faggot-faggot be

burnout in the breeze under faggot-faggot trees
made in the shade be how them faggots-be

(verse 3)

there will never be enough language to know faggots
our tongues are so quick to dispose & show faggots

each morning is a miracle / each day a decision
what value is the past to the tomorrow faggot

we decree our bodies the site of the revolution
all this land is our / manifesto, faggot!

your vitriol / an archaic self-medication
when your quietest desire is to know faggots

we operate with alarm as delicate kindling-fruits
catch our swelling / we dwelling low / faggots

when the last of our spit is wrung from our tongues
all that's bet on the wet will still owe faggots

the unwavering thirst for our extinction / we combust a pollution —
how toxic the atmosphere if there would be no faggots.

Exhibition

when i show you the illicit
behind a fiberoptic veil —
obstruction is a kind of foreplay.
yes — this is an intentional seduction.

this behind is a fiberoptic veil
i build an economy on anything i can.
yes — this intentional seduction
is suppose to be a delight.

build this economy on anything you can.
my taste is acquired, so take your time.
suppose, this is a delight —
the mystery, yours to solve.

you take & taste my acquired time.
take what wilts from my lips —
you — the only mystery unsolved.
i can never stop questioning my mouth.

take all that wilts, my lips.
when every fantasy i try leaves me dead —
i can never stop talking about my mouth.
here, my tongue is bile & tomorrow.

they leave me dead in every fantasy i try —
the overgrown prophecy i am to witness.
bile becomes tongued here & tomorrow —
some end time we have already faced.

the prophesy lives to overgrow the witness.
no future belongs to my body.
these end-times we already face.
my testimony is the absolute of what i know.

i belong to the future in my body —
will truth survive the transmission?
i testify in absolutes of what i cannot know.
what do we make of the delay?

what will survive the transmission?
reveal the half-life of the illicit,
unmake myself as a means of delay
watch for the obstructive foreplay.

narcissus goes to the market

in the wood
the trees say *hey baby*,
so i've accepted my body
can't be both safe & beautiful.

the trees are disheveled
slack-jawed men, backs
on a light posts' lean,
their crotches branching
toward my night-soaked legs.

before i was followed
around markets now
i'm followed out of them.

in the wood
i want my body
to hear itself
between the trees.

the trees are suspicious eyes
& giggles of Black girls
talking fast & light
on the corner, their smiles
like the sky glinting
through an overhang.

somewhere
in the wood
my body is
the buzzing & hum
of the trees.

the trees is the word
RELAX graffiti'd in
white splatter paint
& ungovernable vines.
the sun illuminates the message
like a distress call.

the rain cannot wash way roots,
as both come from the earth.

the wind barreling
in the wood
of no streetlights
teaches me to lament.

narcissus stunts for the void & becomes a flower

i am genius & i won't say that again.
you won't believe me anyway.
what is brilliance in a vacuum?

to think i would be so enamored with mortal bubblings.

before i knew what i was, I WAS, & knowing was the best thing for me.
yet, after knowing what i am, i am, & will be: all i have left.
i am the coagulation of so much wonder.

this body been a bxtch, i just call her one now.

i write my own anthems. make you sing them back to me.
listen to me now but hear what you want anyway.

i almost forget the earth is cosmic too,
that i am hung in the same galaxy of which you claim has no end.

a good night's rest is just a temporal death,
telling myself there's something beyond here, gets me through night.

i have left enough beautiful portraits to remember me by.
i dare this world to take me out completely.

you can't obliterate what never was.

i am as forgotten as i am lied upon.
or i lie to myself in believing,   i deserve memory.
i am made up of all who believed,
or still do; who tell my tale, or will.

in my place a flower will take the poet's eye,
          ashes to daffodils.

prepare the taxonomy for my kind, i will settle in the abyss,
not more unforgiving than the river.

i am made up of all the offerings to the dead. of each season,
restoring. telling myself that there is nothing
beyond wanting to be better than myself,
that i can bloom in the wood.

SIDE B

We Cannot Grieve What Doesn't Leave Us
Or I'll Be at Every Function

The only man I have ever killed lived in my body // At his funeral / I'm in the back of the mezzanine wearing black-jean booty-shorts / oversized white t-shirt / with my own face air-brushed / metallic lavender // I am his widow / & his only son // Below / people are laughing / not weeping / because they are in on the joke // This cathedral / tailored / & fitted for a casket / is a new unspeakable familiar // Safer than mother's heels / was double knot tie / & monogrammed cufflinks // The gag is: even in rigor the corpse smiles // The coffin is rented // The suit mine // All of this is to be burned // He never saw a need for daisies // Drown his ashes in red solo cup / & piss him across the clearing / a mile from the house // If a few could make the journey / if only to listen to the wind / consider that something kind —

At the repast, I dance.
I pink my hands in lipstick.
I shift weight in sea-foam skirts.
There are never enough eyes to question,
if I had always been here.
So when someone calls for me
to reveal
— my trained smile-mouth
lifts the veil —
I perform my favorite tricks again.
Called an apparition so often,
I longed for the familiar ghost.
My mother will tell someone
how I am, now, divine;
That she always discerned
I am a conjurer.
Every prayer required a sacrifice.

I call this look everything I got away with.

In the wake,
I am a different kind of breeze,
in heaven, holding whatever
binds me to this earth.

narcissus reads 1 Corinthians 13, Without Love

The tongue that makes men of angels,
writhes in sounding brass mouth, a clanging cymbal.
Call the gift: prophetic, an all-mystery knowledge.
The faith that this is nothing but removal of mountains.

All my goods bestowed to feed;
my body, to be burned, profits nothing.
This is a kind, long suffering. Never envy the parade.
My lips behave rudely, clenched jaw to not provoke evil.

To require rejoice with iniquitous truth;
if we can call it bearable of all things.
I will cease to speak failed-prophecy
for when that which is real comes that which is dead

will be done away. As a child,
I spoke as a boy, I understood as broken,
I thought as a ghost; but when I renamed this body,
I put away childish things.

In dim mirror, unknowable is how I am often known:
a language abiding in a great & hopeless faith.

narcissus, on kissing

i have learned   to reject
every boy   i've ever wanted to be
on the mouth. no-   body is impossible
but mine is *fucking close to* fantastic.   i imagine loving me
is being shackled   in the cargo   of a dreamboat.
beside you   rages the quietest frictions.
every inch hurts, *no*, is heavy, *no*, *this is not about kissing anymore*,
sorry. i have learned to believe i kiss better in my head.
sorry my mouth   used   to not taste
so coffee-tar,   stale-beer swallowing
tongue still licks   like it should.
I want every-man's collar   stained with the gloss-
smack memory   my lip-shape a body, too.

XXX : Red White And Blue 3

whenever i see a woman alone around faggots,
my first question is:

what is her name?

narcissus attempts resurrection

i.

when the river dries, i allow my need for weeping
suffer a lesser stream   when the wood dissipates

i replant each grave with all the sour-earth i remember
of myself   i accept the absence of air   constantly

amazed by my respiratory fortitude   i dig up all
the daffodils, collect them underneath my tongue

keep my still undying mouth full of a fragrant beautiful
this is supposed-to-be miraculous   i suppose

to be myth   parse out tales told by the self-proclaimed
demigods among us   each will demand a new life.

ii.

the crows are speaking again   they follow me far   i am
tempered to the squawk   talk to myself   suppose i abandon
my need for reflection   let the fates cackle   give the humor
this world deserves   measuring time in disarray   hours
manic into themselves   so try to make my body   time
evaporate   expand   depending on need   in this time
zone   the crows are louder   more glitter under sable spans
i can envy a mean beak   return   a menacing glory

Crepuscular

two
>   ocean-boys
take mile-forest
to the water.
each of different coast.
both remember tastes
of their own baptisms
& the water both their kin.
the sand loose.
this not an
>   ocean. boys
bodies apart
look cross the horizon
for the other-
sides of themselves;
all they see is sunset.
about them a buzzing —
>   oceanboys'
habitat of twilight
bugs & clouds spread
for the last bolt
of sun to glisten the lake,
somehow an endless being.
this tide rises like
>   oceans & boys

watch the sand-line drawn
beneath getting pulled.
this water pulls itself clear & under.
this water pulled the
                    boys'
         oceans.

between each other was a shoreline,
an indistinct hour where light dims
enough to forget this unfamiliar sea.

a coming-of-age

xi.

             my father tried to tell me manhood
        was the evidence in my middle school underwear,
        but i knew of yahoo video.
i knew what safe search meant. i knew i would never find
         illicit temptations in any closets close to me.
i knew that boyhood busts
        into effluvia of shame & relief.
i knew arousal as four-letter word.
i knew listening for footsteps meant closing
        each window to what i hypothesized as myself.

i saw breasts before i was ever told they were bad things.
i remember the starburst graphic over 2am co-ed nipple
        telling me of the going wildness of girls.
i wanted my chest to excite censorship. i wanted to be
        parentally warned against.
i thought being a man was a science
        but learned my dick is so much like Schrödinger cat,
        only appearing when you stare it directly in the eye.
you can't tell me i'm not here, she purrs.

i have never trusted that which grows between me.
i have resisted holding my faith in such a fickle extremity.

51

                    i'd have to cast niggas in white face
to play my high school friends.

i'd allow the white mothers
to play themselves, again,
the ineffectual saviors of guilt
& theater rehearsals.

their fathers
would all be played by me,
touching myself
in the suit worth more
than my last three meals.

i wanted to be a JD Salinger,
more than Holden Caulfield.
& i hated wanting to Blackface
white anxieties. it was all i knew,
the only frustration seemed fragility.

everyone around me is in on the joke:
me trying to pass as more than
fiction beside them.

i was held in constant disbelief.
the unconventional intermission
where the cast comes into the audience
in character & plays along.

that's the humor here,
i know you know
i'm playing apart.
        or i want to believe it,
i want to believe
you know this production is for you.

        xiv.

                i've only been called a faggot to my face once.
        & i knew him well.
in a car driving by me in our suburban downtown.
he was just trying to surprise me. or remind me
i was outside & alive & never supposed to feel safe.
i remember laughing it off, instinctually.
i must have looked so comfortable before.
unassuming. like i could forget the threat of being
called   out.

however: this other time
        i was called a faggot kindly,
without the actual word
escaping across the room.

it was the first day of high school,
in my suburban high school,
a small theater gathering of students
waiting to learn more about the Drama
department & before the meeting starts

among 100 eager eyes,
this chick across the room:

     yo, cutie with the dreads, like girls?
& i have to smile & say no, instinctually.
i had to laugh off my faggotry,
among the audible groans of pale thirst,
& beastial frustration.

granny killed a snake on the way to church
ending in how i became a woman

she was in a hat & heels   because it's disrespectful
for you to believe otherwise   you don't know

how many weapons   slithered past my grandmother
& neither do i.   she would say something like *only God*

truly knows & means it.   it was spring outside Houston,
& everywhere on this side   of The Lord's green-earth.

in my sixteen years   only thing to strike me
in as much fear   was my mother's eyes from the pulpit

& a possum by the fence   on the way to fourth grade.
i don't think i'm scared of animals   so intimately. if i die

by one of God's creations   better one who don't know better.
i say *granny there a snake*   & she say *ok give me a minute.*

the time don't even slow down.   it's like i told her it's raining
& she grabbed an umbrella.   or tell her about my first boyfriend

& she says *that's nice.*   she holds the world like this. every moment
with her is hers.   she has lived in so many other moments, for other

men, taking care of other children, loving other sisters.
          she locks the door.
she adjusts her jacket. she grabs the shovel.   *move back, baby,* she say.

          so i move & she,   as swift as she turned the knob, severed
                    copper-head.
grabbed the devil by its tail   & threw him into the bushes.

          i don't even remember speaking about it after.
          when i got grown i knew i wanted to see a writhing beast in the eyes
    ·   & have time to release him of his own alarm.

the sign on the wall says men lie
& the bartender reminds me of you

he has your beard & i think how long it's been since i've wanted to
   lick it.
we danced your couch around silences & almost touching.
he's goofy like you   but i know how much sweet costs.
you used to make yourself fool before me & all who would gather,
a delicate geek. like you, he appeases the audience.
it is his smile that hurts different. he isn't as nervous.
he knows how much this could cost him. a reality unavailable to you.
he gets food in his beard. he looks like your kind of jest.
on a cloudy day i can actually hear how scared you sound when you
   say i need help.
you are condemning what you cannot save. but he just wants the tip.
the ease at which i can humor him makes me miss & regret you again.
all i never touched, the almost between us. i filled the ever-void —
with a most dangerous devil to toy with. i want
every good night he wishes me.
i wish it was from you, again, away from abyss & quiet.

narcissus (dream 001)

my peace is
always a disarray

in soft light
hours.

to clamor
at rest,

just the way
i've learned.

discard
the tangle.

before
morning.

the moon
claws

daybreak
in the body.

      i need a
      new word for:

if the dead
can't dream.

a wilderness so heavy

write letters to the towers, built
for invulnerability.   not consumed of this world
yet gaze down upon it —
tell of the exhibition constantly unfolding.

imagine heaven with actual castles.
with actual mansions.
actual gold streets & jewels.
imagine a better you in heaven.   already.
imagine being an angel
could also mean being trapped,   like prisoners to the gods.

imagine a better way   to be dispatched to this earth.
tethered to divinity.
better than the ground.
better than this strange land.
this wilderness.
imagine   a wilderness so heaven.

to what sky could the trees possibly grow?   would there be a sun
or suns shining, awaiting prolonged combustion?   to be trapped
in a place where these questions
were the day & evening's plight,   find that joy.   all joy.
the only heaven capable.

narcissus (to mother)

you believed i was beautiful before i did
because you knew. when you told me —
i wished the beauty you saw was yours.
i believe it was, i believe i couldn't carry it;
the way you fill a room. i wished my body,
the expansive extreme, would apply grace
to every crevice & side glance.
how my hands hold your beauty. how they
always say my face does. but your expression
is another kind of freedom i have only seen captured.
you saw me the night i manifested
inside of you. this is how i will always be yours.
i want to be every dream you believed
while others marred them in tar & twisted dismissal.
i want to be the question you refused to answer
in the face of every man who tried.
i want to sit between you & a world that
refuses to praise you. how those who bask
in your grace dwell peacefully in a kind of heaven.

because of you i cannot fear this earth.
what is death when raised by an eternal?

narcissus (for Nemesis)

i've been thinking all week of an offering i would want to bestow / upon you / & i know how deeply you speak to altars / in your temple i have tried to maintain chocolate / mild & black / copper pennies / silver coin / i try to remember sacrifice around you // i've been thinking of all the ghost stories allowed when speaking to the silence / to the flicker of wax expanding / what is a plea for covering than a continued desire for forgiveness // i've been thinking what makes it better / to be thought of / to be presented an offering of personal selection / every altar has its own ritual / its own cocktail of considerations // i've been thinking about myself / before it got me in trouble / but every so often when thinking of you it works / when i am able i will always submit to being at your beckon call / i will prepare open breezeways & kept gardens in your absence // i've been thinking how i brought this on myself.

narcissus, on the new year

this is not the first day
i find myself
unremarkable
& i won't question
why this delights.

my lungs have been
warm vents releasing.

for days now, in quiet
i still never attempt to fill,
to sprawl, but this morning
i see my traces around.

remind me that i leave ashes
in hallowed seashells
& soaking pots in the sink.

i cannot be weightless,
so filled with water, soaked,
in stillness. overnight.

we marked ourselves
returning & i hoped
this would not be ventured alone,
or i hope more could have
marked this journey, again.

A Future Yesterday

we was dancing, like we could let all the breeze out our lungs,
sounded like a church, like the one down the road with no streetlights
behind the second lot, then abandoned.

the trees didn't scare us no more, weren't no more blocks to burn effigy.
just all of us taking turns smiling back and forth,
a concert, a gathering across a main drag.

you can smell the grass & gasoline & frying of peppers,
& grease. it didn't matter when you got there
just as long as you didn't miss the band, in all white.

a host of beat-box soul, there the saxophone sweetened
the bend in the back of our knees. we knew that dust
wasn't gonna rise without our shuffle atop it.

the earth finally swallowed all the graves into itself
& sprouted wings & jean shorts, & neon body suits,
riding around on technicolor bicycles.

you couldn't see nothing but the crackling
of the present. couldn't hear nothing
but the night finally time un-afraid of its shadow,

the moon stopped boiling blood,
remembered how we always been its creatures
& when the second sun rose we sang to her too.

told her   thank you for the land again,
all our blood been the keepers.
this rapture was a home-going back

to ourselves. it didn't matter when you got there,
as long as you didn't miss, the generations of abandoned lots,
sprouting streetlight revivals at the end of the world.

even the sea stayed quiet there,
made way for our bones to again quake & holler
— all this, a joy

Babylon

After Ajanae Dawkins

i.

        freedom is probably a rapture,

available   only

to those who believe.

        reimagine

                the fear of being left behind.

what is power

        if the entire land is damned?

could we even know liberation here?

      if we bodied the revolution over land or

      landed the body in revolution or

      revolted the land we call our bodies —

the tongues we fought as borders

cannot   easily

                be severed.

there is no prayer for the Tower of Babel.

to whatever divinity has scattered us as such:

        what will we make of our new cradles of tomorrow?

ii.

        the issue of decolonizing the body:
the limited imagination we are offered
past the ships leaving the shore.
what happens to our mouths,
when the last shards of ivory finally flow out,
spitting all back into the ocean.
will our bones begin washing up out of the sea —
a railroad mob of salt marrow? we have never
completely known the expanse of the deep.
we have continued to build obelisks
in the sky to hear what to do with our ritual speech.

For Drought & The End of the World

I remember how summer storms
are still a natural occurrence.

Again, sun breaks the afternoon cover.
Again, light thunders the air thick.

So, when this terrain is a known-desert,
this drought is not all the lungs can muster.

Thirst is this kind of devastation,
a cracked earth, dust blistering:

an endless land lingers to the shore.
Every Pacific Ocean birth gawks at the fault-line,

the dwindling flowers in the valley.
Stakes grounded set wildfires of the dead —

because every kind of hysteria smokes beyond the hills
& every kind of anxiety hangs over the palm trees.

What if it was too late to replenish the beaches?
Would the jagged rocks already be in the sea by then?

All the gold swallowed back into the pan.
All the islands submerged as mountaintops.

The remnant cliffs would finally exhale,
swallowing them-selves no longer.

Again vultures, instead of the ghosts
burrowed in the foothills & barren rivers

          & atmospheric pressure
kept by imminent quake & deluge.

narcissus (unplugged)

i worry i have so romanticized loneliness,
that the content with my reflection
feels as much like a freedom as it does not.

what if i truly wither away without touch?

i turn everything into a poetic,
but i imagine all of this is conceding defeat.

i hide longing in a metaphor
& it becomes warm enough to rest in,
but every desire can't *blossom* or *shutter* or *wallow*.

maybe i use my reflection as distraction.
make my own body a shimmering thing.

someone once told me:
>   "the anthropological reason we,
>   as mortals, admire jewels is because
>   we are drawn to water
>   & how light reflects."

i have an obsession with precious things,
so i have fundamentally never loved my body.

we are not to look outside of ourselves for validation
but my reflection requires my full attention,
lest i compare it to another.

i am so easily distracted by a luxury.
i imagine every-body else has something i don't.

but i have me?
i have something some-body else desires.

what if the only thing i can hold is myself?

my best-self is fleeting.

i keep hoping the river will let me make sense of this vision.

i was born to never know all i could become.

another poetic excusing me from myself.

i worry less about dying unknown than alone.

i worry my worry is its own kind of arrogance.

i am just trying to see what everyone else does.

i am more confused than enamored.

i hope to die knowing my mystery will become myth.

thank you

— to what I know as divinity manifested on this earth, *my mommy*, I always begin & begin with the ways you blessed me with language.

— to my sisters, Janessa, Blair, Tafisha, Bree, Yah-Yah, Emani, Yasmin, Xandria, Angela, Tori, Candace & the Girls, & all the Black women & femmes of color from Boston to Detroit to California who have lovingly steered me to the best & most possible truths.

— to the homies, [redacted], Casey, Ocampo, Roy, Julian, Brandon, Derrick, Golden, Kayleb Rae, Colette, Sara Bess, Kiki, Lyrik, Rebecca Lynn & Rawhide Father, each of you in your own magnanimous ways have tempered me into a better self.

— s/o to my first Black Therapist, Dr. M, you helped the river not feel so murky & to leave the echos where they lie.

— to the wilderness I was blessed to find myself in, *Detroit, Michigan*, thank you for holding me in the ways that you could & I wish I could have held you better.

— to any & all who could, or care to call me kin, again I am elated to shared this work with you.

acknowledgements

"I Know I've Been Changed" / "a coming-of-age" & "For Drought…" appeared in *Yes Poetry*

"Put Your Hands Where My Eyes Can See" & "narcissus stunts for the void" appeared on *Big Lucks*

"narcissus #17" appeared on *The Shallow Ends*

"Manual" & "narcissus in dystopia" appeared in *Duende*

a version of "interlude (day beat)" appears in *Shed Every Lie*

"Lyrebird" & "We Cannot Grieve What Doesn't Leave Us" appeared in *The Wanderer*

"Exhibition" appeared in *Hyperallergic*

"narcissus goes to the market" appeared in *Nashville Review*

"narcissus reads 1 Corinthians" / "narcissus on the new year" & "Babylon" appeared in *Fields Magazine*

"i am interested in the Black condition" appeared on *TAGVVERK*.

BONUS TRACK

i am interested in the black condition.

Or

The Dark State
The Ebony Shape
The Sable Order
The Circumstances of Owning
    the Complete Absorption of Light
The Opposite of Regard
    for Safety or Well-Being

—

there are so many ways to condition:
control, govern, touch, treat, prime,
temper, acclimate

there is no way to be just black:
(see alternatives: *coal-black, pitch-black,*
not-white, dark, absent of)

—

like hi, ummm ru following me too so we can chat? im looking forward to your book whenever it arrives. thanks for putting art into the world
20:49

your creativity is inspiring
20:55

sorry i'm not sure who you are
20:55 ✓

figure a — Screenshot #1
The Black Condition
is a creative inspiration,
to someone else.

ASK TWO DIFFERENT NIGGAS "WHAT IS THE BLACK CONDITION"?

Struggle. Pain Perseverance.

Unlike • Reply • 🖒 1 • 1 hr

A stomach full of baked man and cheese, colard greens with hamhock, and cornbread 😊

Unlike • Reply • 🖒 2 • 1 hr

figure b — Screenshot #2
2 Black Conditions

The Black Condition is making resilience easier to swallow.

78

Black temper / Ebony rage / Sable fury.
Temper Black / Temper Rage / Temper Fury

Black acclimate
or Blacclimate
or Black-Climate
or Black ocean

evaporates into the Black sky &
Black rains down to the
Black Earth &
Black grows again.   oh

the dying of Black Earth.

Black control,
govern Black ,
meaning the Black
be uncontrollable
or Black be
ungovernable
condition the
governed Black
controllable.

Black touch, touch Black, touching Black
to Black, a Black touch, a touch Black
treat Black as Black, a Black treatment.
Black prime, primed for Blackness, priming
Black, the prime of Black.

figure c — Screenshot #3 | Triptych

The Black Condition

is selling your ass

because it is art.

I ADMIRE YOU GUYS.

you're gonna be exposed

20:59 ✓

just thought ide drop in and say hi and see if you wanted to chat, I like twitter friends

wait, u dont like me either? sigh, I just like art

trying to be friendly

I got both your books, when the second one come at least. I admire you guys.

21:01

A collective of Black[s] cannot be a Pathology.
We cannot be a construction of unmade things.
I wanted to call this work "you're gonna be exposed" but in exposing you I'm exposing my own condition. I'm conditioned to make sense of pathology your eyes, your mouth so interested in The Black Condition,

The Black Condition, here, meaning ten years of Black dick in your mouth convincing you I, too, needed to know what your mouth do.

The Black Condition is your mouth, white & wide & famished, needing a reason to make demons from all of which you feed.

figure d — Screenshot #4 | "friendly"
The Black Condition is
still symptom of white admiration,
I don't like it any more than you.

81

WHO'S MAN IS THIS?

FOR REAL, WHICH ONE OF Y'ALL NIGGAS WHITE BOYFRIEND'S IS IN MY DMS?

NAW LIKE I WANT THIS WHITE MAN'S BOYFRIEND'S NAME IMMEDIATELY.

I NEED TO SPEAK TO HIM NIGGA TO NIGGA.

I NEED TO SPEAK TO HIM NIGGA TO NIGGA

Collect him. Collect your man. He slipping. Your imaginary leash is too long. He loose. He speak out of turn. His mouth salivating again. He sees the wrong snake. He's not immune to this venom. Collect him. Before he get himself hurt. Before he gets exposed. (too late) But who you? How ya man get this far, who told you his dick was gold standard gagging the wealth seeping from your skin. Collect him. He who wants to cure your disease. It's a way of being that he wants to siphon from your cock & i've known mouths like his, they are never satisfied. Collect your man. I can't tell you how to sleep at night, I can only hope you are haunted by his flesh, him silver spooning you out of your body. A decade of chocolate & dirt browning his teeth. I hope he eats you whole, devours your need to be consumed. i cant tell how you sleep at night but I have laid next to ghosts a woken dead beside myself. Collect him. He's buying your brothers. He's buying bodies that look like yours. He lights your ass on the fire of his torch. You are the monster he wants to call intimate. His interest is in your demise. How much do it cost to kill you?

MY BLACK CONDITION

an obsession with language for the impossible.

a fear of my mouth giving away my fear.

my mouth being a spectacle of its own right.

meaning my mouth as truth teller & body pleaser.

meaning my body pleases whether i like it or not.

my body is my body where i like it or not.

my condition is believing my body could be mine.

my Black body is mine most in my mouth.

i condition my body to obsess over itself

make Black a necessary fixation.

tell me i'm impossible & i'll show you

my lips. my condition is a language

i hope you never learn how to figure out,

your mouth will forever be fixed wrong,

there is no dialect for wandering eye,

or wet mouth. & even here I have given

my condition to your gaze. caught

in your interest. i am obsessed

being seen when i am told

i am invisible. when i am

told i can be held, treated.

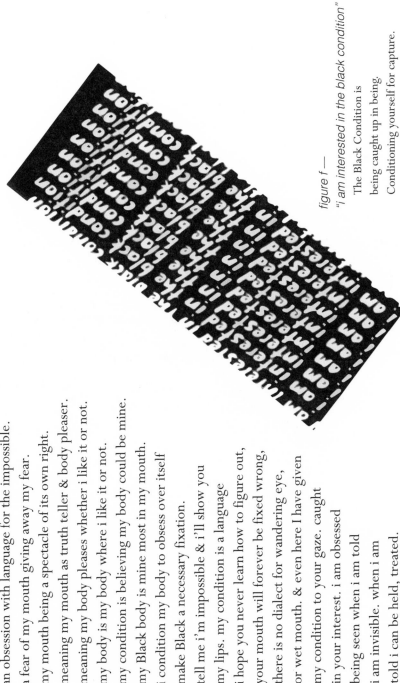

figure f —
"i am interested in the black condition"

The Black Condition is
being caught up in being.
Conditioning yourself for capture.

83

jayy dodd is a blxk trans femme from Los Angeles, California—now based on the internet. they are a literary & performance artist. their work has appeared / will appear in *Broadly*, *The Establishment*, *Entropy*, *LitHub*, BOAAT Press, *Duende*, The Poetry Foundation's *Harriet Blog*, *Teen Vogue*, & *Entropy* among others. they're the Workshop Director for Winter Tangerine, editor of *A Portrait in Blues*, and author of *Mannish Tongues*. they've been a Pushcart Prize nominee and co-editor of *Bettering American Poetry*. they are also a volunteer gender-terrorist & artificial intellectual. Find them talking trash online or taking a selfie.

Nightboat Books

Nightboat Books, a nonprofit organization, seeks to develop audiences for writers whose work resists convention and transcends boundaries. We publish books rich with poignancy, intelligence, and risk. Please visit nightboat.org to learn about our titles and how you can support our future publications.

The following individuals have supported the publication of this book. We thank them for their generosity and commitment to the mission of Nightboat Books:

Kazim Ali
Anonymous
Jean C. Ballantyne
Photios Giovanis
Amanda Greenberger
Anne Marie Macari
Elizabeth Motika
Benjamin Taylor
Jerrie Whitfield & Richard Motika

Nightboat Books gratefully acknowledges support from the Topanga Fund, which is dedicated to promoting the arts and literature of California.